The Sandpipers

The Sandpipers

SELECTED POEMS (1965–1975)

With a Foreword by
Richard Eberhart
and a Portrait of the Poet by
Edward Plunkett

David Posner

A Florida Technological University Book
THE UNIVERSITY PRESSES OF FLORIDA
Gainesville, 1976

A selection of the Virginia Commonwealth University
Series for Contemporary Poetry

Walton Beacham, *General Editor*

DESIGNED BY GARY GORE

Library of Congress Cataloging in Publication Data

Posner, David.
  The sandpipers.

  (Virginia Commonwealth University series for
contemporary poetry)
  "A Florida Technological University book."
  I. Title. II. Series: Virginia Commonwealth
University. The Virginia Commonwealth University
series for contemporary poetry.
PS3531.07642S3   811'.5'4   76-13586
ISBN 0-8130-0549-3

Acknowledgments

"The Body," "My Body Like a Cockroach," "In Memory of W. H. Auden," and "Norwegian Spring" are reprinted by permission from *Esquire Magazine*; copyright © 1974, 1975, 1976 by Esquire, Inc.

"Love Story" is reprinted by permission from *Evergreen Review*, vol. 7, no. 30, May-June 1963; copyright © 1963 by Evergreen Review, Inc.

"Dialogue with a Dead Marxist" is reprinted by permission from *Four Quarters*, vol. 22, no. 4; copyright © 1973 by La Salle College.

"A Dialogue with Variations on Wordsworth," "The Shapelifters," and "Portrait of My Father" are reprinted by permission from *Kayak*, nos. 11, 14, and 37; copyright © 1967, 1968, 1975 by Kayak Books, Inc.

"Penelope in Bayside" is reprinted by permission from *The Malahat Review*, vol. 36; copyright © 1975 by *The Malahat Review*.

"A Poem for My Wife Strictly about the Weather" and "Lessons in Natural History" are to be published in *The Malahat Review*, vol. 37; permission for prior publication was kindly given by the editor, Robin Skelton.

"Requiem for Celine" and the original version of "When the Company Left" were published in *The Mediterranean Review*, vol. 1, and are reprinted by permission; copyright © 1970 by Robert DeMaria.

"The Mirror" and "Middle-Aged Flounder" are reprinted by permission from *The Mediterranean Review*, vol. 2; copyright © 1971 by Robert DeMaria.

"In David Hockney's Studio" was published in *New American Poetry*, edited by Richard Monaco, reprinted in *The Logic of Poetry*, edited by John Briggs and Richard Monaco, and is reprinted here by permission; copyright © 1974 by McGraw-Hill Book Co., Inc.

"Incident at Wellington," "On a Recent Protest against Social Conditions," "The Campus," "The Birds," "The Education," "Terni," "The Suicide," and "The Sandpipers" are reprinted by permission from *The New Yorker*; copyright © 1961, 1964, 1965, 1966, 1967, 1968, 1972, 1974 (respectively) by The New Yorker Magazine, Inc.

"Puerto Rico" is reprinted by permission from *Perspective*; copyright © 1966 by *Perspective*.

"In Memory of Captain Marryat" is reprinted by permission from *Prairie Schooner*; copyright © 1965 by the University of Nebraska Press.

"The Great Auk" and "Indian Architecture" are reprinted by permission from *Quarterly Review of Literature*; copyright © 1965, 1972 by *Quarterly Review of Literature*.

"On a Renaissance Painting" is reprinted by permission from *The Sewanee Review*; copyright © 1969 by the University of the South.

"Todi" and "On Leaving the Clinic" are reprinted by permission from *Shenandoah: The Washington and Lee University Review*; copyright © 1965, 1968, by *Shenandoah*.

"Lecture to the Geophysical Society," "The Townsends' Japanese Rock Garden," and "Jamaican Ministry" were published by *Saturday Review*.

"In Memory of John Berryman," "In Memory of My Grandmother," and "Elegy for Harvard" were published by *Minnesota Review*.

"North" and "Himalayan Journey" were published by *Chelsea*.

"Conversation with an American Landscape" was published by *Salmagundi*.

"Medieval Dialogue" was published as a broadside by the Lowell House Printers in Harvard Yard, December 1966.

"A Song for Innocence" was published by *Encounter* and reprinted in *The Rake's Progress*, published by the Royal College of Art, for illustrations by David Hockney.

"Major Corbett's Bedtime Story" was published by *The Kansas Review*, and reprinted in the *Borestone Mountain Anthology for 1968*.

Other poems in this collection have appeared in *Antaeus, Choice, Epoch, Kenyon Review, New Letters, New Mexico Quarterly,* and *Poetry Northwest*.

For my wife
OLIVIA
who gave me faith, hope
and charity

Foreword

I like a certain fiery charge one gets in reading the poems of David Posner, a sense of nervy aliveness in the work. It is of a man looking widely around him in astonishment, who has the ability to register on the reader's consciousness the incorrigibility of the plural. He has a compressive force to make manyness into an artistic unity through complexity and diversity reduced from wideness and variety to discretionary attitudes. Intelligence communicates content and form in immediacy charged with litheness of expression exhibiting selfness of style. Sometimes his deftness and niceties have a Moore-like tendency.

One receives depth of thought here, wide-ranging experience not limited to this continent, perceptions not limited to the present, words fused in a kind of psychic freedom to new uses, new communications which mark the startling poetry of Posner as deeply stained beyond rhetoric with essential meanings, man's condition, fate, and possibilities directed by will and necessity to new poetic extrusions and makes.

He is a slipstream in which an acrobatic flyer cannot help going straight on.

RICHARD EBERHART

Contents

The Sandpipers

The Townsends' Japanese Rock Garden

This speckled granite
bare except for pachysandra
is Fujinoyama, Fujisan.
A piddling fountain
satisfies invisible
sheep, a
wandering ghost or two, the
dabbling hands of
the boys Jackson and Rhys
who rest in shadow.
A few strips of bark
are folded into wings;
moss gathers perfume
perhaps for birds.
You can touch stonecrop,
a fleshy herb with cymose
yellow buds hot
like the sun. The eye
observes
holes, furrows,
variations on
a possible flute;
clipped bushes above myrtle,
sand beside mowed grass;
a branch pokes the edge of
the sky
as if to pry it open.
Whatever the willow
does
it does not mourn.

The Sandpipers

I count nineteen pairs of legs on roller skates, thirty-eight
  delicious blades of grass,
  with patches of hard sunlight piercing the interstices,
  casting invisible shadows
    on the waxed surface of the
      sand.
    They sway as if blown by wind,
    they pirouette, they
      genuflect
      at the edge of the froth.

It has taken me a week to figure out what the sandpipers'
pliant bills
    scoop
    from the crevices
    between—say, an infinitesimal
    fracture of a nautilus and
    a scarab
      or an agate
      the size of a pinhead—

yes, even up from under two grains of sand.
  What could you want smaller than that?
  Maybe it's their eyes alone that perceive
    delicate snails,
    whorls of algae
    wrinkled like a minnow's eyelid;
      if, balancing its wings on the edge of the ultimate wave,
      a sandpiper got a sudden yen for stars,
      then God help the furthest star.

But I imagine they keep their nights for sleeping
since they never stop from dawn till dark,
   whether it ebbs or flows,
   attacking the tide,
   retreating so precisely at the last moment
      that I'm sure they'll drown below the crests.
      They never get so much as the
      ribbon of their toes
         wet.

When I observe in the fire of light
   their curved Venetian feathers sparkle,
   I imagine the entire ocean bearing down,
great hulks of waves splintered from the sky,
   trying, from the depths of the sea,
   to follow their tiny knees.

Major Corbett's Bedtime Story

It had rained earlier that day.
After the rain stopped the leopard
Stiffened his whiskers
And crouched like a runner at the beginning of the path
Leading to the thatched hut between the rocks.
The girl was opening her door
To squat in the moonlight.
She turned her back to him. Belly to ground
He burrowed in weeds,
Sidled a trunk, and sprang;
Then cradled her toward a terrace.
When she was dead, he held her up so high
No bruise showed on the fragile earth.
He carried the corpse a mile in cool air, down
A twelve foot drop, across a valley to a cave
Where he undressed her.
He ate the thigh, the breast,
Licked her from the soles of her feet to her neck.
Folded her body just past the flowered entrance
Under a willow among virgin foliage.
If you had stood on the edge of the jungle
When the leopard stretched out his paws and slept
Beside the green girl humped like a stone,
You would have thought the innocence of evil
Matched by the evil of innocence;
Her monstrous peace, her midnight,
Her long grass, her delicate hair.

Himalayan Journey

A climber told me when you climb
You have the mountain pulling at your feet,
Loose rocks, an avalanche of snow,
A sudden storm, darkness.
Boulders touch your knees.
You dance for the pleasure that lies
In holding your balance:
A sparrow lightness
While the body's weighted down;
Always above you, the mountaintop drawing
A man's death carefully to scale
So he knows where he stands.

Lecture to the Geophysical Society

The Russian said it was no dream.
He charted two magnetic poles.
He studied the weather as it rode him on
where submarine mountains divide the ocean—
the floor of the sea furrowed like hell.

He watched the ice-pack thaw at spring
till he could stick a spade inside it;
Ocean frothed through the holes he cut
to let the melting snow away.

The blackboard showed the shape of wings,
how ice is propelled.
Often in storms there is no peak
in sight, no place to go but down.

The soul can sink
or float, according to the instruments.
There are no islands in so cold a heaven.
Ice is not earth. But still it will bear life.

The Mirror

for Patrick James Omweg

The flesh stripped off these bones
They stand akimbo: a tree without leaves,
The branches white,
Holding their own against wind.
If a slight movement shook you now,
Who'd think of you among the branches?
The best one might lean toward—
Heartless under his winter sockets—
Is what you hoped for anyway:
The old dream of a man turned to stone.

In Memory of W. H. Auden

We know that line about the ruined children.
All those orphans longing to be fed
Have ages ago popped off to heaven. You said
They would. What else did the children do
When you got them to bed and when
The innocence they never had
Drove you into poems so pure in wit,
So full of the flesh and bones of
Your still compassion: what could we complain of
But not being equal to such love
Or more than the briefest partners of your insatiable
Intelligence that left no stone unturned
Under which a finger squirmed or an eye flickered?

If Kierkegaard could see you now
What would he say about Washington Heights?
Would he smell the Ischian wine, the unwashed sheets;
Raise his eyebrows at the thought of Vienna
And then remembering it's finished, the scarred, rocky
Landscapes folded away on the shelf forever
And the sea returned to Caliban its rightful owner,
What sort of *nunc dimittis* might he scribble?
It must have been Verdi you played
For the peace of those last long Oxford hours
When you rose, shuffled to the window,
Leaning toward St. Aldate's to catch the chimes;
That map face hovering like a question-mark: Into Thy Hands?
When your wrinkled fingers began to close the door
They'd still leave it slightly ajar,
So someone special could always enter.

Woodpecker

His starched ruff has the iridescence
of the fleck in the iris of my most exotic friend
(inconspicuous enough to be triumphant).
A hundred yards off, at the Mall pileated hardhats
hammer and tar the rooftops
till every small bird in the neighborhood is smothered.
This hot wind smells of singed feathers:
red for our blood, black to hold us together
in a flash of burning.

The Birds

It is difficult to imagine how vulnerable they are,
these sleek heads, yellow-eyed
(an observer would call them round- or pear-shaped).
They dip into grass, somehow
chirrup while holding a worm in one corner of
a beak,
make waddling through milkwort
irresistible
(and not funny).
The feeling my skin gets is
iridescent,
nothing in me except what shines on the outside.
I understand their pleasure
at putting one claw after another
in identical gestures
(or using their wings
to cross the quick spring clouds in this
suburban acre of thick
traffic and skinny trees).
The weight of my body belongs
to the earth and moves
up and down.
The sun lifting my hair
drives me west
into a darkness full of wind
and the bones of sparrows.

A Stranger in Clare

I

The rooks calling from a field behind the village
never expect an answer:
they turn and turn in the air
till they drop out of sight.
This is the house, two cats guard the window.
My wife and sons live here.

I I

A wing of rain folded in an eighteenth century gutter
opens, ready to rise
toward the half-sun.
I see the park;
children crying from a swing
kick at my eyes.

I I I

No music anywhere:
loneliness hums
like a housefly caught in my hair.
I'm thinner than grass.
I am a stranger
returning to the scene of his crime.

I V

I ought to wear a black
cloak and be invisible
when I cross the street, bending
on the bare places, slipping
against the gate.
What's the body but a guilty stare?

V

I keep looking back over my shoulder:
nobody's there.

A Poem for My Wife Strictly about the Weather

The forked sun strikes at my ankles,
steams from the red mouth of an oleander.
Its fragrance burns my nose.
I walk on fire up to my knees;
swim in water the rest of the way;
kicking an old stone in a blind lane
uphill, till it rolls down again.

This house has no termites,
silverfish, dryrot or mildew,
though it can rain so hard
through the bearded oaks against the louvers,
doors and the pages of books
stick,
and the knuckles of my fingers
counting the months since you stayed behind
glisten wetter than cheekbones.

Do you remember how you shivered among
those drifts of snow piled deep inside the skull,
the miles of flakes you crossed between two faces
gone white after the cold and the silence?

What's real about the climate isn't pain.
It never freezes: the wind doesn't hurt.
If a man had nothing better to do with his body
he could lie naked in the light all year,
a golden brown from ear to ear.
I stretch out straight and dead;
and unbutton my shroud.

On Leaving the Clinic

for Randall Jarrell

Randall, the toothless slum, the dog scratching
The sunken porch, remember. So does the widow
Wearing her sticky weeds; the salesman retching
In the alley; and God the quarterback casting his shadow
On the sidelines, calling the signals, catching, fetching
The ball with a dog's innocence. When they hit the meadow
The game's over. But you knew all the rules,
What simple voices fed the animals.

Love was their beautiful cage; handshake of a word
Would do the trick, your face in the dust sharp-eyed
And sometimes blind with anger. Gun-shy I heard
You beat the bars for justice when men cried;
Their wounds opened, they aimed down the air absurd
Bombs at a neighbor's village. Someone died
Always beside the truth. Scanning your verse,
Waking in pain, I listen to the hearse

Rattle past my window. Not yet, not yet.
The driver smooths his hair; but adds, soon.
Light bears my loss, each day's immaculate
Landscape. Wind blows, stirring the magic stone
At your heart: a feather floats. The sun has lit
Our knowledge, saved the sky: we stand alone.
You saw the earth turn black from star to star
Across the cold nights where you raced your car.

I've hopped the clinic. My strange madness flies
Like a late autumn bird to join the flock
Going south for winter: I duck the cries
It throws from the horizon. With any luck
That bird is gone for good. I'm stuck with eyes
But without wings, I hope. Money for my sock,
A few words for my page are all that's left.
Change me, the world whispers. It was your craft

That won. I lie on a bench here in the park
And count my syllables and trust the swans
In the lake nibbling my childhood down their stark
White necks (a chunk of bread, some raisin buns,
The wrapper from a Milky Way) have dark
Secrets to tell. If I could change my plans
Today a swan would sing me all of death.
Sister, I watch you glide. And hold my breath.

My Body Like a Cockroach

for Theodore and Elizabeth Friend

I frighten it out of my mind and onto the washer.
It scuttles down the sink,
Each of the legs remembering
As they run: hide me.
This cockroach stitched in brown,
Once you get over the freckled skin,
Nostalgia of the garbage bin,
Is a large handsome creature.
Of course, its nature
Is dirty.

Elegy for Harvard

for Mathilde Mortimer Heller Argyll

Knock, knock: who's there—
casting his shadow on Claverly Hall?
It's me, the dust, my dears,
rising from your belly.
I'm potted among palms:
ignore my bald pate.
The trick is to go west with grace,
speak softly,
carry a big stick for the Dark Place.

We were wild and smooth enough with wings
tight as we glided down the corridor
night after night. Our presidential janitor
clutched his pince-nez, sick of counting swans:
my roommate was the wisest bird,
a Jesuit outwitting Cambridge;
"You lesser Phoenixes, behold Adonis.
Bow to my beauty, please."
We heard the clapping of the trees.

When Mathilde hocked her diamond,
she sang about the categorical
imperative: I. A. Richards climbed
mountains, Matthiessen watched the cold
sun from his chair.
Handsome Bill pulled down the shades.
"I am the law, I am the Ace of Spades."

It rains, the room darkens:
whose light enters the dead mind?
A young boy rattled by wind:
can anyone tell us what he feared?
I remember how Mattie praised
the Holy Ghost in the *Wings of the Dove*.
Then died of love.

Names come backward now
like an old maid's parlor game:
Mathilde locked in her Scottish castle,
Pearl crouched beside her mirror,
Bill dancing on broken bottles—
dreaming of Tennessee's moustache
as he leapt under the train
to the music of his wish.

When a crane ripped down the old Howard
I wept for Harvard then,
those Founding Fathers resurrected
among forgotten friends:
eyes, teeth, feet
lost in the tumbling of a house
where burlesque queens and soldiers used to meet.

Love Story

We lived all summer by the Sound. The cook
Baked huge raisins, my nurse afraid of the sun
Read movie magazines on her bed. I played
Under an elm in the garden. There were no women
To watch me, only birds. One day at twilight
Vivian pissed in the air like a young boy.
When winter broke, free to do as I pleased,
I walked in the park to find a girl with breasts.
The child holding a Bible against her womb
Said, do you want to read it? I ran home.
Mother took me to England. On our ship
A pink and green lady wearing bells
Locked me inside her cabin, groaned, no, don't.
That hot August a platinum taxi-driver
Picked me up at Shoreham-by-the-Sea:
"Ducky, I'm mad about babies."
In Paris the Countess gave her usual dinner;
I was John the Baptist, my blood burning.
Frightened, I saw how beautiful she moved,
The unrelenting eyes fixed us on a platter.
Hard men obeyed a wink, presidents, bankers.
In her castle at Aix I went from room to room,
Touching the velvet, staring at rococo landscapes.
Love must be different from these
Flowered walls that copied the leaves outside.
I could not tame her, I left her in a rage.
Then came Raab, the docks at Copenhagen,
Kornhamnstörg, Dianabaden, an island
Off Naples; the baths at Rome which closed
When two boys locked an old man in a steam
Box and beat in his head. Somehow he had
A pencil on his naked body and wrote
Guido, Giovanni did it, before he died.

Suffer

This bird knows the answers.
Flying between the sun in my eyes
And the sheets of snow which cover the alley
Sometimes he sings for the hell of it.
Sometimes he's full of unpleasant silence.
Now he beats almost at the bedroom sill
As if his wings were going to fracture or freeze
Unless I opened up.
It's hopeless to guess where he is:
Shall I let him in or let him out?

In Memory of John Berryman

How long did you wish you were a knife?
You couldn't scrape the wound away.
Man, this flesh stinks, Life for a life,
I hear you say, and your tongue slicing the air
Fine enough to hold the pieces: look
There, *there*,
This is my body:
So down—how far,
Not even sharpest of your words veer
Toward the shadow—it hurtled, falling
Till you were the only word, for all that hate,
You could not tell the weight of.
Yah, said the 9:00 wind. Splash, splash. Who's calling?
Henry's liver heaved
Under the ice at midwinter.
The crowd waved
Goodbye (a few leaves clapping at the center
Of the river) and where that yellow
Balloon plunged, being partly air it floated
Back up in a white morning
(Good fellow, Henry. We all voted
For him), surfaced, spilling
Bourbon and blood.
So you cracked your last joke, a rude
One, filling
The lungs with its ripples.
Dear police, have you come to gather
Hank's bones? A wife and sober friends
Squint barracuda eyes. Hands
Will be fins and
Tears father
Rocks in your river as they try to move
Off, leave Henry's waters
Behind for the sake of love.
But can't. It's prison, prison

All the way home through our years
(They fears his poems—
They has reason).
They drown on dry legs;
And you with your wry (I mean bourbon) face
And your smashed skull
And the holes in your tube.
Finish. The cold settles.
This is my body;
Treat it well, Massa Death,
As the cube rattles at the bottom of the glass.

Incident at Wellington

Just outside of town in a white lace
House with mansard frills, Grandfather had rung
Three times for custard. You could hear the parrots
Chortle in the aviary, peacocks
Calling "Nell," the blowing of doves. Genteel
Trees brushed the tops of louvers. A dog with a bell
Tinkled across the pumice to Greenstone Hill.
Along the long bay window, bicycle shadows
Bounced from the road. A limb of oak rippled
Among the marble. Grandfather looked angry,
The maid in tears. "I'm sure I'm sorry, sir.
It's the pudding on the kitchen porch
Won't set right; there's soot around the edges."
Grandfather leapt up, dashed to the garden.
Dawn seemed rising out of the moonlit sky.
"Call the engines!" The chimney was on fire.
Orange by the time the firemen came,
His wooden mansion made a circus cutout,
Tongues of flame laughing from paper windows.
The attic fell, the rugs and curtains caught;
In twenty minutes all that Victorian splendor—
Tasselled chairs, the carved settee, portraits—
Blew on the lawn in cinders. The metal door
Which led into the aviary stuck;
No one could open it. The birds died screaming;
Wings, feathers seethed; obsidian eyes
Dropped upon the sanctuary floor.
      Fifty years have passed. My grandmother
      Has a jewel case filled with lumps of coal.
      "Diamonds and amethysts," she smiles;
      Puts her head to one side like a bird
      Listening to the crackle of distant footsteps;
      Will not sleep in a room with a shut door.

In Memory of My Grandmother

She balanced heaven
On an old woman's varicose legs.
"Teach your grandmother to suck eggs?"
God in his time, yes, but even
A ninny had better fish to fry:
Her daughter's comfort, feeding the avocado,
Combing the dog, trying to answer
A thriller about London thieves.
She twisted the pearl on her finger,
Took off her corset and stays;
But would not turn her face to the wall.
We buried her in a cemetery so brutal
It might have been her last joke:
To crack among the plastic flowers.

Requiem for Celine

for Annette Herr

A servant at fourteen
From lentil soup to burnt coffee,
Stuffing the chicken with laughter,
Basting it with fresh scandals,
"Who wants mirrors?" you said.
We loved your crooked body,
The beady bones that made a
Scaffolding against the raucous air.

Eight miles from where we used to dance
Round and round the kitchen clock
They buried you at Fontenay-Aux-Roses,
The cancer in your breast
Opening like an enormous flower.

For Lily Pastré

Those parties, those beautiful parties.
Last night I flushed them down the drain.
The sound of running water made me sick.
I won't be going out again.
The year's finished, a cold rain dirties
This hopeless sand that sticks to my wrinkled heels:
The echoes curdle, light returns
To guide the ball under the wickets on your lawn.
It burns across the Mediterranean
A pitiless glare that withers castles,
Cracks our suburban chatter. Nadia in a turban
Has washed her hair, Dolly staggers up the beach,
Peter rides his silence like a horse:
Your children, sad and well-bred.

                      Cicadas reach
G♭ with their wings: the terse
Indifference of the dark takes over.
I have tried to be clever for your sake,
Though you rarely heard what anyone said,
Buttoned your dresses crooked, stood enormous
Enough to fill any room. We had to move
Aside, asking that formal disarray, was it love?
Now your Spanish terrace pokes its fat finger
Between the trees, the sun rises through your house.
Here in America five thousand miles of water
Blaze toward your dead window.

To Hurt

for Charles Micarelli

A kind of hurting digs in like a tree.
It doesn't feel hot
Or shake much if a storm's coming.
It can stand for hours while the sun darkens,
Lean through the night, not hearing voices.

No faces pass on the other side of the window:
You crouch, your wooden eyes go blind.
Whose house are you in?
A mouse is scurrying behind the wainscotting.

You touch glass, you stare: somewhere
As easily as a bird
The mind flies without the body
Or is it the body moving again?

The Suicide

I drink this whiskey from a window overlooking the sea,
The fierce plunge
Fixed at the back of my skull.
Bicycles roar like breakers down the shore.
In twos and threes the riders disappear,
Taking my life in their wheels.
Gulls scream as I dive.
Oh, fish, have I hated enough?
Let's sleep in silence. This is no dream.
The birds have murdered the trees.

In David Hockney's Studio

Jean Harlow's nailed in the alcove,
Her belly bursting like the bloated
Flowers that don't make a garden
Five stories above the beach. Shall I jump?
If I land in water, I'll swim awhile.
But it's rock from here to there.
A black cat stands on white steps below us
Licking her whiskers. The hungry portrait of
Mr. Isherwood lies trapped
Between his bowl of fruit and his withered books.
Who will write a prayer for Christopher
Like old Soutine with his butcher's eye
Lunging at every passing saint,
Hanging himself every week on his hooks,
Drawing blood from a piece of rotten meat,
Until each maggot turns into a fly?
The snakes are singing around my feet.
Goodnight, David, I'll write the way you paint.

A Reading of Flickers

for William Masselos

Evasive as any gentleman
One foot or the other is always dancing.
The text's as virtuous as an Elizabethan battle.
Every time he preens his tail
The Spanish Armada gets ready to sail.
When she dodges his stride
Ambassadors step aside.
They have, of course, a lover's point to settle.
Yet neither ruffles a single feather,
Wings folded: no singing either.
We say they move to music
Like Shakespeare remembering his lines in the mirror
Or Sir Francis Bacon climbing out of his carriage
To stuff a dead hen with snow.

Litany for a Dead City

in memory of Lily Pastré

I

He built innumerable
      temples
      relic-shrines
      houses for Buddhist priests:

            101 dagobas
            476 images of Buddha
            300 rooms for the reception of images
            31 rock temples with
            tanks, basins and bushes for the holy
            230 lodgings to accomodate travelling saints
            50 halls for preaching
            230 apartments for the use of strangers;

and lakes so huge they were called "the seas of Prakrama."

When he had repaired four thousand canals and waterways
he said a special prayer and
took a young mistress into the mountains.

Everything you could think of was done to make Pollanarua beautiful.
Rising from the brink of the vastest of his lakes
the city settled on its eyrie like a snowy egret;
you saw in the absolute whiteness of the waters
reflections of white palaces
coated with cream-colored cement more polished than marble;

hovering in between like lesser birds
the gilded spires and cupolas,
golden umbrellas.

To the right and left of it, rich from stretching
both arms in a yawn of pleasure
the fertile land leaned into the sun,
pastures crouched half-awake on their haunches,
groves of flowering trees, palms
curiously careful if the wind blew,
clumps of tamarinds casting the coolest of all shades;
and ficus whose branches bent in the manner of gentlemen at table
listening to their neighbors.

Prakrama playing on a drum surrounded
the city with an immense wall enclosing
an area about thirty miles long by twelve wide.

At the four gates he affectionately commanded
        almshouses to bless the poor
        hospitals to bless the sick;
        carved oblations
        to bless the memory of how men suffered
        (the way butterflies move their wings).

Inside, even the smallest streets were called
"noble" by the ambassadors.

You could study in academies
        conservatories
        assemblies
        libraries the color of old men;
or inhale your body in public baths as pleasant as gardens.

Prakrama's palace, seven storeys high, contained
                              four thousand rooms
                              a thousand granite recesses
                              vestibules
                              staircases
                              statues of beaten gold
                              chairs of beaten gold
                              gold-encrusted tables
                              beds of gold
                              studded with rubies.

In a bed so large it was like a field of red poppies
Prakrama, loved by his wives
                              mistresses
                              children
                              his servants
                              soldiers
                              farmers
                              fishermen
                              silversmiths
                              horse traders
                              his merchants in their bazaars
                              whores in their balconies
                              his judges in their chambers
                              tigerhunters in their tents,
laughed.
A fixed starlight burned from his eyes
as he went to sleep
thinking of his Empire.

I I

It is strange to consider so perfect a city,
capital of the island for five hundred years,
suddenly
   abandoned
     to "utter desolation".
In the course of incessant wars (according to legend)
enemies must have devised means for
cutting off water:
the feeding rivers were diverted.
Millions whose existence
     depended upon
       the rice crops
may have been reduced easily to starvation.

Either they died of famine
    or fled in fear
      or were compelled
      simply
       to leave.

I I I

Once the inhabitants had gone
the downfall of the city would be swift;

legions of white ants would
reduce the woodwork to powder,

rain would blacken the gold,
sun split stone;

insidious parasitic plants
taking root in a million crevices

would develop overnight
into trees,

rend the outer and the inner walls
                              the roofs
                              the pavements
                              the fountains
                              the stairs   the steps
                              the pipes   the columns
                              the obelisks
                              the giant hands made of jade
                              the jacinth eyes
                              the alabaster feet.

Herds of wild elephants would do their part in
hastening the collapse of tottering buildings.

I wish I could imagine the astonishingly rapid
growth of thorn.

Elephants and the luxuriant vegetation
have hidden the

emplacement for
upwards of seven centuries.

Except here

      now

            to hold back
            the jungle

                    at this mourning which
                    is not brief either
                    in the full and endless green of your death
                    where I build my temples.

In Memory of Friends

Some streets have familiar names
As if they had taken off their clothes.
All of them arrive at a dead end.
The passerby says, meet me on the corner.

   When I get there, the houses have gone away,
   My footsteps follow the same inscrutable
   Inflections of goodbye.

As usual I cross
City limits. The stranger slowing down
Is rain, night.
Solicited by my shadow. The

   Eyes of dawn
   Open
   Incuriously
   Into light.

The Education

for Graham Binns

One day, old specialist, you drive
Your car aimlessly through the countryside.
Someone waiting with a long smile
At the stop sign to flag a ride turns out
To be yourself, the boy you started with.

How can you answer a life full of knowledge
Which leads to a day like this, the wind perhaps
At half mast, leaves falling, late flowers, a line
Of oaks gone red and the familiar
Passenger you thought you had forgotten?

In Memory of Captain Marryat

When we shipped the dead lights
What was the use to man the cats, cast anchor?
Where did the bumboats hide, fresh girls
Who used to sprawl between fore and aft,
Waiting to get drunk on our Madeira?
Five hundred miles away in the sun,
While broken waisters groaned on the orlop deck:
What we reefed was blood, the riggings howled,
The mizzenmast all bone against black teeth.
We caught the futtock shrouds, tightened the stays.
You might as well say God Almighty
As in these storms haul taut the weather brace.
We were brought up to hear our fathers pray,
Young within sight of the spars.
A punctual heaven waited like a convoy,
Brass-polished cannonades in order.
Now comes the prize, what made us take to sea:
In manus tuus. And the sloop goes down.

Dialogue with a Dead Marxist

for Tobias Rodgers

"The guilt that arises from what men do is small and scarcely compatible
to the guilt that arises from what men fail to do."—Christopher Caudwell

1. We always travelled away from the sun
    to be rich like God
    and inherit ourselves.

    The darker the stairs the clearer the dream.

    I draw the curtains as I climb
    holding the light back,
    increase a moderate speculation.

    Here is a sack of grain
    estimated for Thursday
    when it has gained three points.

    I am stained from buying dark northern Spring
    (Nu Tone high 26½ low 26),
    flung headlong by a zealous nightmare
    into the Proletarian cellar
    under the expensive carpet.
    I walk so quietly
    the cat grows jealous.

2. You rode to death in a soldier's lorry.
    Marry? you said.
    Keep up a wife and home which read like a
    book full of patience for the middle class:
    'poor dear muddled so-and-so,
    solitary, discontented, ambitious.'

3. Yesterday I cleaned out the attic, found your
      volume on the decadence of culture
         which sounded like a love letter
         now after thirty years:
            "You don't understand anything,
            mysterious, arbitrary in your gestures,
            Imperialist in the war,
            liberal Fascist, you
            loathed the workers,
            denied Marx,
            proud of your eclectic mishmash:
            psychoanalysis, comparative religion.
            You refused to grow old,
            always kept my house away from your house,
            never liked crowds;
            no genuine furniture in your room,
            only a picture window."

   Darius, my sad Persian, whiskers and all,
      is it really you
         crying at night in the vacant lot?

4. Once upon a time the odour of a rose
      preceded the rose;
         or if people could see reason
         as one sees a flower at midday.
   Now I sit indoors
   casting no shadow.
      A redeemer in a glittering aeroplane
      will put things right from above.
         Only the dead overthrow governments:
         the rest of us go on living.

5. What beating of wings
   thought makes:
   returning to the nest,
      hiding in a tree;
      no possible action
         unless you call a tree
         a social necessity.

   Today I slammed the shutters,
   wrapped in a thick coat;
      marched against snow,
         my route in rough weather
         a few straight phrases
         warming themselves inside me
         like the chances of an early spring.

   Your ghost began to stir again,
   carving a Spanish epitaph:
      here lies my heavy blood,
         it flows down the mountains like water.
         It is lighter at last than stone.

For Adrian Wedgwood, Drowned at Sea

Escaping from some outlandish prison as rough as God
You were always breaking your fingers, splitting your skull,
Climbing a tree too high, falling
Down Welsh potholes, down mouths of caves
To a central light in the darkness.
Locked inside a reticence more solid than a German castle
You had special information the Ogpu wanted.
But you slipped between two words with a smile.
Often well-dressed you dreamed of
A Japanese girl whose eyes moved so slowly
They kept time to your silence.
Then you wore your hair long, your clothes dirty.
Everywhere you went the secret travelled
In a suitcase jammed with whatever you owned.
You crossed mountains at a dangerous season.
The woods were on fire when you reached the coast;
The sea came howling from the tip of your tongue:
You knocked once more on the grey world like the body of a fish.
The spar cracked your head open;
And threw you home.

Terni

for Marian Chigi

In San Pietro five flushed saints
Stare at Christ's plastered heart,
Will the stitches come apart?
The chancel steps drop down in alabaster
As I rise toward the light.
The Spada, high with small square windows,
Frames a nun in the doorway.

From a street full of broken teeth—
Crooked roofs in a blind alley—
I wander toward Buozzi for an ice,
Across rails beneath a half-built house.
Where does one go before dying
Except to watch the traffic slide?

One day a year the waterworks turn on,
The falls toss rainbows in the air.
Farmers whistle from the park;
Old women in black silk whisper
Eighteenth-century prayers among the crowds
That drift to earth, caught in a cloudless spray.

Todi

for Mary Broquedis

At 5 o'clock when I could just see the papier mâché
A film company had set up beside the campanile
A shutter banged open and a Tuscan voice screamed,
Mario, Mario, you'll have to go out to get water.

I grew tired of hearing the cocks crow in the middle of town
And the policeman who coughed in the archway all night
   rattle doors
Which made cats jump and dogs bark from behind a wall.
A last stopping of the floodgate held me, a pause in the song

Of birds. Then silence lurched, the storm of day broke in on
My sleep like an angry drunk. My toes stiffened, my dry
Mouth pressed against the bed to count the cries of
   the waking;
My nose breathed new bread and coffee, garlic and cheap oil,

Guessing what jobs people smelled of and what crimes were
   burning on the stove.
I might as well have slept in Corfu till the bugle raised
   the king's flag
Or whimpered at the Saloniki trolley that crept along the white tower
As hungry as a German truck rounding up Jews from a seaside

Villa, or turned on my back while the bells of the monastery
Played below my window at the Montalembert,
   shaking the monks
Till they tumbled out of their cells, still sleepy
   from midnight Mass;
Or yawned down my white Edwardian mornings at the Cavendish

When I could still listen to the Negroes leaving
   the whorehouse behind

The carpark: my mornings in Marrakech when a woman yelled
With joy, weeping, or a wild animal sniffed the garbage.
Now again I felt the animal crouching under boxes
    while peddlers

Unwound carpets, growled and clattered pots and boiled
Mint tea. At Istanbul cobblers began to hammer
Before the moon set. I could make out the fat
    shape of riverboats.
The tide of feet from the Horn to the street where I stared

Receded among the cleats of Buffalo football players
Leaving cold bars after dawn and across wet stones to get
Three hours in bed, dreaming and drunk and spread under sheets
Moving in the promiscuous light. Tomorrow I'll get up

At sunrise in Rimini in the shadow of Sigismondo's lecherous
Church and with fingers like centuries the girls will carry
Baskets of fruit for someone to buy and the boys
Sell combs or stumble toward the factories.

Old women will dust off their daily benches with a blank
Smile and take out their bread. Then it will be time
To go to the station without a word in my head,
Half asleep, and catch the train for another city.

On a Renaissance Painting

for Edward Plunkett

Look at this mother, the wise virgin holding her child:
A pitiless innocence that asks
To be satisfied, though the whole world suffer.
Do you suppose it is love she finds in his face,
A way out of herself and into a landscape
Where her feet will not echo among leaves?
In his smile the flood of her torment
Begins and ends. She knows the use of rain,
How lightning strikes. A tree grows at her right;
The sea behind her shoulder mirrors the sky.

The Pageant

for Patty Estep

You see them inside the tapestries at Cluny,
Each in order from green to gold,
Faded but still so perfect
That a world you were never promised hovers,
Beak and claw, over the hard pavement,
As the outstretched mind in the stony
Corridor shifts into the sun.
A blast of remote fanfare
Suddenly pierces the complacent light.
Unhooded your eyes spring forward,
Isaiah the falcon, catching a voice from the grass;
Or high enough to teach the hunter tricks,
An equilibrium between murder and grace.
It might be so only in history
Or in childhood perhaps, but it was so:
That balancing of threaded hawks
On the wrists of harriers among their prey;
Every leaf visible behind them:
The wings real wings, ready to unfold.

distraction of a kiss
                    in due season
luxurious branches filtering
wisteria lavender hollyhocks
                              petals matched against time
                              sweetness of honeybees
                              in the arbour
drinking the ascending spirit
whose art of hunting fishing falconry
"the instinct to kill that achieves intimacy with the life of nature"
remembered exactly in every motion
                              the promise of salvation

a gesture
creeping like orange
in leaftip
fringe of spray
                    whitening sand
infinity of tongues
                    evolving a language of decoration
symbol of heaven bending
down to
my claws
marked with the stigmata
under the frozen crust of monastic calm
God's blood
the dormant green
behind the clarity of created form
transparent Trinity
trefoils
dripping
on leafy capitals
in margins of manuscripts
a face upturned to the east

past blade   stem   lip   bough   wing
to whatever invisible
                              music
around whose harp and halo
angels dance
like food bubbling in the kitchen pot

Holy Mother   for this
fallow garden   the body
passionate at our feet
these vermin   lean flies   our mad
children   Blessed Mary
because of our running sores
flesh ravaged in your name
we count our beads in pleasure
marking the black sins white
on painted walls where
"many figures I see
hell on one side   heaven above it"

North

for J. W.

"How then would these philosophers ever leave their cave?"

I

Ice is
the color of perfect stillness.
One does what one has to.

I I

Learning, for instance, the best way
to be fleeced when dead;
it's not necessary to cut open
a fox to skin it.
The legs are freed and the skin pulled down over the fox's head
like taking off a shirt.
This fills the hut with a revolting smell
but saves the mess of blood.

I I I

The steamer tied up at the coal bunker
to fill her hold.
A last puff of black smoke
from her long funnel

told you you were headed
toward Spring.
The cliffs had a familiar smell,
moss beginning to bloom with tiny vermillion flowers.

Though frost lay on the hills,
the rivers poured melting snow into the sea.
Rain hung in the air,
green on the lower slopes.

At that promise
you turned away
blinded by the sun;
heard the glaciers crack in your skull.

I V

I am north enough,
what grows in me grows bare:
I am rocked among floes,
a refuge for the puffin's eye.

V

And the epitaph always under water:

HE CAME TO SVALBARD
THOSE STRANGE ISLANDS
FAR NORTH IN THE ARCTIC OCEAN

BETWEEN THE LONG DAY AND THE MIDNIGHT SUN
HE FELT ON HIS BODY
THE POLAR DARKNESS
THIRTY MILES FROM LONGYEARBYEN
BURNT BY THE SILENCE INTO
PERFECT WHITE
HIS DREAM: OVERWINTERING.

V I

You read on the smooth face of the tundra
desolation:
your blood sang as you froze;
one rock mountain after another
split by glaciers—
the grip of the ice
reminding you ironically of a white hand
extended in friendship.

V I I

A question
         the size of a
                  blade of grass
remained unanswered.
             Listen.
                A clatter among the stones,
a movement
         which touched the flowers
                       into life—

so that an Arctic poppy
                bowed
                          for a moment in the wind
as though a delicate stem
                  could hold
                          its shape.

How much would you give
                  for the ingenuity
                          of man?

Occurrence at Owl Creek

for Paul Sobka

The gun prays for your body as it aims at
An easy bird crouched under a tree,
Longs to comfort the lonely woman on her bed,
Pour an old lady her red wine.

Meanwhile back at the gas station the boy
Holding the knife in his stomach rolls over
Against the cornfield at the other side of the pump.
A saint blows off on his cycle, shouting God,
Having adjusted the Chinese border of heaven
For fifty dollars folded together like the wings of
Sleeping angels: their veins hurt.

The boy's eyes are blue.
They stare, wide open, into light.

The Campus

I work to music on the radio.
The one discordant note comes from growling
Dogs up on the hill; police brought them
To find a satyr after dark who tries
Climbing in windows, waiting behind trees.
The trees are too thin. I suppose he sees
A skirt flutter over the hill, then runs toward it.
The echo of his steps drops dead on the grass,
The logic he meant to push gets tangled in his feet
And flaps like a loose cord inside his windy skull.
Smooth skin reflects the moon, his trousers crackle
Like dry leaves. His hands perform a game
On the victim. He can bite her lips,
Stifle the cry, kiss, jump away.
He may want to kill her out of pure joy.
Probably his wish sails in a child's park,
Traces a flower with a red crayon.
It's easy to imagine his young body,
Tough-limbed, hairy, lurching from side to side,
Panting to get out of the dark—

                              By day
The campus here is pleasant. Health Science,
The Art Forum, throw cantilevers at
The broad steps of the Non-Sectarian Chapel.
The rituals of this climate keep us busy.
Men trim the privets, move snowplows in winter.
Bells whine every quarter of an hour, domestic,
Complacent; but beyond the clock tower at times,
When the wind is cold and the night falls early,
A question bangs in our heads like an old door
That will not stay closed, for all our knowledge.

On a Recent Protest Against Social Conditions

The maples have turned. Fire snaps on my tongue,
Veined in red, a brief felicity
Which hangs in balance between speech and silence,
Trembling toward a word whose simplicity,
Like wind, everyone has heard.

I want to write a petition, make a prayer,
Get somebody punished, rewarded.
But the birds in this academy
Refuse to sing by ear, they take cover,
Since light is an approximate hope.

The Dean can tell dates, balance a budget,
Explain education. Although his nerves are on edge,
He is clear about what needs to be done:
You must know facts. The sun
Has nothing to do with these.

The Dean would not like shifting among shadows.
You speak against injustice; it alters
Before the mind can hold its shape.
Imagine a crooked elm disguised by sun,
A tree that rots in blossom.
The hue and cry must be begun again.

And after all, what is it but a tree,
Always almost impossible to describe,
Pleasant in summer,
In winter barely visible on dark days.
Do you call a tree an injustice?

I see in the branches ignorance, corruption,
Murder in its season.
There are other names for the cold wind
And the uncertain color of leaves.
It is not knowledge that knows.

Truth will drive the scientist to prove
His facts before the elements agree, and love
Can find a definition
In all sorts of weather. We die together,
Caught in the roots of evil.

Suffering was never an exact science.
So I speak when I'm hurt or when
You are, though I don't know the reason
And cannot be sure there ever was an answer.
Only the dead say nothing,
Even then not in fear of error.

The Tourist

You could always sail farther East in a black ship,
Though you had to take off your trousers to please the moon:
One way of keeping the light in order.
But myths come expensive these days.
Of course, the brochure includes love. You can plan
A night on twenty dollars or murder
A rich old woman out of curiosity
(And disappear in a bus of sightseers).
When rape's easy, you strip a thousand years
To the bone, clutching a few bare facts.
As usual, the special season for violence
Is on page 8, under "reduced rates home."

Puerto Rico

for Vincente Geigel Polanco

Inexcusable Candado doors:
conversation at a 90° angle
in a room haunted by sardines.
The singing cod up inside my head
push me in: look at
the dancing and later take a girl.
You want to hear your money laugh.

A rump in black silk shifting from side to side
looks Cuban but not political.
A nice day survives history,
my shoes enter your poverty;
hard light on the shanties at water level.
We're rich, will that be good for love?

The argument ends with kissing all around.
You are right, I am right,
the best the trellised arches can do
is shelter lizards
sleeping on fine louhala
planted under McKinley.

A stone puts out her tongue.
The weeds groan.
This is the place against the cliff
near the abandoned tunnel facing the sand.
The sea casts a vote in favour of love;
the wind says yes until
there are no women, only voices.

Oh Princessa!*
the prisoners waving their cocks
murder us in our dreams.

*the name of a prison in the heart of San Juan

Conversation with an American Landscape

for Joachim Murat

The cage in which it suffers
has no doors.
It learns freedom by shifting
the position of the legs.
You blind it
to make it sing
(if you own a bitch,
paraffin the offending part).
It is sometimes called
the New World, usual
yet somewhat improper title
America.

"Sir, a race of convicts."

Franklin declared it the cruellest insult:
emptying English jails upon the colonies
reminded him of his mother.
Old Bailey archives branded
felons week after week,
thousands transplanted for more years
than many poplars grow.
Popeham invented the plan of
sending crooks as founding fathers.
Each plantation was very like England
"being spit out of the very mouth of it."

My mother had blue eyes, my sister fair hair,
my brother's cheeks were apples.
My mother worked hard but she didn't die young.
My sister was tried for a witch.
My brother died rich but he died in prison;
four cousins in Philadelphia, not very smart.

I remarked the gentility of American women,
small heels, fine silky hair,
delicate and marked eyebrows.
"Oh that is easily accounted for.
The women who were sent in early times:
public women are always good-looking."

The hawk's beak at the sparrow's tail
gives you a good round sense of geography:
to Pennsylvania, Maryland, New York, Boston
they banished offenders
driven out of the common "jailes,
a readie way to furnish us with men,
not allways either with the worst."
Divers young people had been twice punished and
not reformed:
when I woke
the walls woke with me
(a puking junkie groped the guard:
for Christ's sake, turn me on).
Steel bars across the door
spanned continents
like money in the bank.

"John Armstrong, Elizabeth Armstrong, alias Little Bess,
Richard Bennet, Brannan, John Brown, Hugh Cambell, Elizabeth
Camphill, alias Cambell, William Carnegg, John Coghill,
    Henry Colee,
Mary Caslin, Catharine Cox, John Cross, Eleanor Davis,
    George Emly,
James Emly, John Haines, James Hobbs, Thomas Jones,
    Antonio Key,
Thomas Macculer, Martin Nanny, John Payne, Thomas Petit,
    Luke

Powel, Daniel Ray, Elizabeth Roberts, John Rogers, Mary Row,
Thomas Taylor, Anne Todd, Jane Vaughn."

You know your ancestry is accessible
by means of American genealogists
who go abroad to trace
the lineage of Bostonians.
You ride behind steam;
the landscape, respectable, fades into a
card game, the knowledge that
order breeds order from
convicts who were
political.
You recall someone who worked for your father,
domestic service by a lantern-jawed
old man: picked up tips on the stock market,
retired a millionaire at eighty,
married a local slut;
the Social Register at eighty-five.

I speak now with the voice
a stone makes
if you kick it,
how a majority are always dissolute.
Near a puddle of rainwater
they caught me at the end of a passage,
slid handcuffs on my wrists,
threw me in the cell for ten hours

flayed by questions,
racked by lights,
gasping at the end of their rope,
a corpse they kept from
crying.

The Bristol alderman over his shining pate
wore a bright new wig.
His broadcloth friend the magistrate
preened damask breeches,
ruffled his copper cloak lined
and trimmed with black, smoothed
his virtuous black stockings:
"It is a shameful and unblest thing
to take the wickedest of people, condemned
to be the people with whom you plant."

Every animal knows his father.

Look, a bird sleeps in the rain.

On truant plains, the home of bald eagles,
men charted rivers, pursued by
Indians, promising themselves gold,
a meeting place for the mind and heart
where history was wildfire
and niggers avoided questions.
The simplicity of this statement has never been outdone:
how one had been sold by sheriffs to shipmasters
who would contract

to carry a man beyond the seas.

Wigs were denounced as an arrant cheat
to lend criminals a respectable appearance.
"Ran away from Reverend D. Maghill,
a servant clothed like his master."
Having absconded so far,
his antecedents unsuspected,

69

Henry Justice (sic), Barrister at Law
who stole books from New College
became tutor for
George Washington.

We found that cursing helped,
pleasures of heaven filled the stews:
"May the devil make a ladder of your backbone."
An Indian summer on the coast
we bedded down among
"these confounded natives, serangs,
lascars, quartermasters."
Irish officers fleeing to the continent
we dreamed that cows were licking our feet.
It was hot inside each head
when widows and orphans shipped as slaves.
Mother of God was all they said.

The company declared it would accept no man
who could not bring a testimonial
that he was moral and religious.
Which is like saying no man
not of good moral character
shall be licensed
to keep a saloon.

They worked the way birds fly,
rapidly by instinct,
crouched when night overtook them
empty with
fever, wounded on cliffs,
parched on the high seas,
thrown to the mercy of

sharks. Our
drivers beat them in fields as far as the ocean.
If they remembered Eternal grain
sown in their blood they reaped
the chaff, a price for two arms and two legs,
slavery instead of prison:
to be used until death.

The Body

I

We used to break stones in the longest road
I ever saw: hotter than home.
I was the youngest.
I said no, when the guard got me under a tree,
No, though he pushed me down.
The leaves rattled like snakes.
I had just enough time
To pretend someone was crying.

I I

When they fished me out of the creek
First they thought I was a stone,
Then they thought I was an empty bottle.
But everything worked out okay: they found
My number sewn on the back of my shirt.

The Mansions

for Melissa Banta

I should worry   I should care
I should marry a millionaire
He should die   I should cry
I should marry another guy.

I

1918 was a fine year for military handbooks,
utilitarian as salt and pepper,
the table set plainly;
knives and forks democratic,
civilized blades with strong handles;
stiff napkins based upon
a family whose father must be General:
no arrogance but
Dad spanking his son,
a simple punishment
to make intelligence glow like a five-cent cigar.
Men died according to the rules,
a method into the heart performed so well
you might call them invisible
like the City of God.

I I

On the Bay expensive keels inscribed their hieroglyphs.
We ate our meals inside a golden hexagon.
From the credenza to the valance Tiffany-hooded
Sconces fired a scrolled epergne.
Fingers plunged in peacock fingerbowls,
Threw ermines across Gothic thrones.
Mary Scanlon, who wasn't a nun yet, let me come down

To shake hands with twelve Corona Coronas and twelve
Fleurs de Rocaille.
Father slapped the terrace door open, pointing his Pharaoh chin:
My son, in every one of these yachts you see
A beautiful woman wearing her pearls.

I I I

To keep death delicate,
The chivalry of hands from stinking,
We walked up Stanford White's great dazzling banister
Into a ballroom built for a thousand pairs of gloves.

I V

A seagull planes the horizon,
dust drifts till it flattens at my feet.
Father, I'm home,
turn on the lights: in the wind
the big houses are rotting like newspapers.
Up from the caretaker's abandoned windows
columns of sparrows rise into the Egyptian night,
their wings brief, incurious, cold.

Portrait of My Father

My mother's friends had big breasts and played bridge.
Her gods were Jimmy Walker, the Duke of Windsor.
When she cried, Father bought her a bond.
On Riverside Drive the cold wind in the winter,
The white-faced summer screaming of the nurses
Made life unfashionable. Lawyers, doctors,
Executives of clothing stores moved east
To Park and Fifth but worked late hours,
Never got home in time for anything.
They paid their bills, played Sunday golf at the Club.
Went twice a year to synagogue, their pews
Expensive like the smell of good cigars;
Subscribed for classics in imitation leather,
Tried concerts, lectures, exhibitions;
Sent their wives to Europe,
Never kept a mistress or got drunk,
Having faith in their women
Painted and pointed like Gothic apartments
Shaded by Tiffany lamps.
Though Eddie Cantor wrote *Caught Short*
And bankers leapt from seagreen windows,
My father held his head above the water
So loud-mouthed and so proud
No one knew how nearly he drowned;
Name-dropping at dinners, lived on credit,
Full of the "speed, alacrity and despatch" of wit;
Threw his weight around like a bull-terrier,
Never stopped wagging his tail:
"My friend the Mayor", "my friend the Governor";
And Lillian Russell's fan.

He gave us a house with black swans on a bay;
Grew blind, talking about Theodore Roosevelt.
I never saw my father weep.
When Mother left him
The hair in his ears thickened, his wrinkles got deep.

I I

The moon is almost as old as my father.
Hidden behind his craters
that stony presence colder than wisdom
turns me toward the light;
a promise on his dark side
keeps me imagining life where no life is.
He shows a hollow face
I can't touch with the eyes of the heart.
Father, in the waxing of my blood
I watch you wane.
Please, be kind for a few hours.
The empty sockets stare, the thin lips freeze;
The scowl among the furrows won't let up.
He sits fixed in his green chair,
curses me quietly night after night,
moving from west to east
in a little less than a month: and does not die.

When the Company Left

for Rick LaVelle

I

I used to own this house
In the days when jungles were fashionable.
I know what it means to
Dawdle into mahogany or cedar
Like a closet for holding clothes.
I lean against the sill, a false dawn
Upsetting both the stars and the sun.
That rose bush is still blooming:
Petals covered with snow.

I I

Waking, I see the guests have gone,
Dish skulls piled in the sink.
I'd better get away into the hills.
What's the use of running?
I live here: mosquitoes win.
Kenya's like that, you squat at twilight
Drinking your whisky under a cloud of flies.
Fever is fever. I sit it out
Dance after dance.
If only the heat would go away
And leave us together,
We who were once lovers: my bones and I.

Middle-Aged Flounder

The blinds are drawn
to keep the rugs from fading.
Sometimes a shark's moon
rises at the edge of the curtain,
circling slowly without anger,
a dead fire.
Cold on the silence the suburbs roll;
far off, the bad men in the boats
promise a whale
wounds the length of a man's arm.
Poor fish, what harm can you do now?
An eye on your underside looks at hunched seaweed
as if leaves were the food of love.
That light fixed in your head
could swim for the sun.
But it's too late to change a habit:
sleep now.
Your body grubs among holes,
as one might say of a sinner,
goes deeper into darkness.

Suburban Storm

for Anna Russell

Birds look down
Out of clean roofs.
This dull town
Has a big clock.
I count the steps
From trim shops
To neat trees,
To ponds, tea trays.
Clouds open
And close like doors.
Lightning moves
Without love's
Anger or a giant's
Hate, a thunderous breeze
Bends a bush, a scarf.
I walk outside,
Inside,
No grief higher
Than the thermostat.
The brief
Storm sets,
Rolling the flats,
Direction north
By east above the earth.
These facts agree like wings
Caught on the wind which swings
Butterflies from the lane.
It seems they are blown
As far as Finland where
They die in the cold air.

Penelope in Bayside

for Gary and Dorothy Clark

I

Day after day the light
Grows more domestic behind her picture window,
Purrs at the hearth. A dull moon
Repeats the kitchen sink:
Love, love, love when the tap drips.
What strange adventure, ambergris floating on water,
slips through her fingers
As she scrubs an expensive skirt?

I I

She watches murder with music,
Till the late news sends her to bed:
In her room whales hang on a calendar;
She circles them neatly.
A clock stands under the crucifix.

I I I

If a saint stirs from the ashes of her mind,
It is always the memory of someone starting to yawn.
She combs the hair of falling trees.
Behind her door even the mirror sees
She has forgotten whom she's waiting for.

A Dialogue with Variations on Wordsworth

for Mark Bryan

Once in Carolina I
saw half-lit with sun
a clenched poppy the size of a man's
fist raised straight from the
middle of a field: water
cut one side, hills
shut the other.
At the touch of the flower
I walked into my shadow:
I met a life
grown out of grass,
pointed at the ends.
I whirred among cattails
until I reached the river,
circled the hills.
These limits caught
the edge of wisdom.
I climbed, I waded
between a trill of light
and the first spills of
darkness on the blades.

A red bird lands on a red field
across petals, then
up. He is wide
open.

Wings take to water,
petals hinged on a stem
cover the ground.

81

Now flowers move everywhere
in a sparrow's dream.
The day must be
enough, the cheep of impending
darkness.

So much birdsong
lasts as long as
a cloud falling
in rain: the call
from grass and water
shakes the furthest wood.

My territory stands at sundown
a flowerless red with a stone
around its neck.
Drown, old beak, drown.

Indian Architecture

for Tom and Caroline Stacey

I

After all, wasps
Have the best sense of architecture,
Hollowing their hexagons.
The difference between inside and outside is
Inside, it is cooler:
Lignum of the god enshrined in red sandstone
Making the gesture of the lotus as if
No exit out of stone was possible
Except from stone into more
Stone:
To penetrate into the heart of a mountain.

I I

A fragment catches
The rhythm of the whole temple.
Who is he, the figure dancing,
Shoulders in flight,
The broken head
Leaning out of prison?
Shiva perhaps, lord
Of light, beneath him
The demon. Clearly
Order is produced from chaos,
Good from evil when

The princess looking out
In between the pillars
Will move back into the space where
Meditation becomes repetition.
A stairway climbs with infinite ceremony
Among the fronds or against
The mountainside.
Everywhere in India these ruins resurrect
Celestial musicians
Cool above the heat of the sun.
Their legs flex like animals'
Legs, reminding us
Of butterflies or dragons.
The artist must have measured
The distance from hell.

III

Although Vishnu tortures
The impious king, his veins
Do not crumble.
Arising angels handled
In a profuse and witty manner
Repeat themselves like blades of grass.
Repentance at intervals
Has been reduced to
Tanks, baths and gardens:
192 rooms in which to offer flowers.
Doors open, the rain growls,
A casual perspective of lions
Beneath whose claws
Marble cannot survive.

84

Lessons in Natural History

for Peter Nathan

I

From Siout to Thebes for fifteen days
my greatest joy was shooting where they basked.
They taste like lobster:
Arabs who eat camels' flesh
refuse to eat a crocodile.
Herodotus tells how you catch them with a hook:
the Bible hints it's only God who lands them.

I I

Turks love vultures:
the one and only original harpy,
her wrinkled face polluted,
a black beak covered with gore;
sacred talons
useful in removing carrion.

I I I

Irascible's an understatement:
more choleric than an eighteenth century toe enflamed with gout
a chameleon certainly doesn't live on air.
Projecting its eyes a long way from the socket
it eats a dozen flies in fifteen minutes.
If the dark green gall's

transmitted into the blood
it turns to a livid coal.
Paroxysms of rage
shake it at a touch.
When I took away its eggs—
the size of a coriander seed—
it died.

I V

(a)

Cerastes coluber, the horned viper
holds virulence beyond belief.
I bought mine from the *psyllē*, serpent catcher:
diminutive horns no larger than those of a snail,
hardly three drops of venom
under two hollow teeth in the front of the jaw.
Talking about the nature of poison
a surgeon-barber swore the most deadly came from
the "mucous membrane of the intestines" of man.

(b)

To explain how a snake could walk and talk
before the curse was given
a Hebrew scholar proved with joy
nachash once had two meanings:
it wasn't a serpent but
a baboon who tempted Eve.

Either he surrounds a winged globe
representing the architect of the world,
or biting his tail he
gives an exact idea of eternity.

This is how I remember India:
a serpent in the hand of every god.

Invariably chiselled erect on Egyptian temples
he may have been worshipped for his wisdom:
probably to keep him from getting angry.

In Nubia I watched him stand
five feet off the ground
making circles.

No snake is fabulous.

V

Worse than an asp
its venom exudes from the feet.
Men of Gourna watch out for
watermelons where these geckos crawl,
often tie one by its tail—
a piece of glass placed underneath—
flog the tortured lizard till it discharges
poison on the glass.
This poison has no use.

V I

When I dragged him near the hyenas,
my dog went mad with terror.

They dread a man: slink out of sight.
The desert's covered with the bones of their victims.

Water angers them.
They never eat by daylight.

V I I

It comes from Ethiopia
when the Nile floods:
Abou Hannes, "father John"—
plumage grey, wings anointed with black;
size of a pigeon.
Once, the Nile dried up,
flying serpents filled the air,
until they were eaten by God:
put to flight by
a flock of ibis.

V I I I

For character and looks the jackal's
in between fox and dog;

loves caves.
I found one in the Jews' Alexandrian cemetery,
gnawing a human leg.
Every tomb I visit
they "dispute the entrance."
Their cry at night's so full
I often mistake it for the lamentation of women
at the moment of death.

I X

I heard the sky black with locusts.
They always travel in a straight meridional line.
"The land which is before them is as the Garden of Eden;
behind them a desolate wilderness."

X

In the narrow passage of a subterranean tomb
I saw the sparkling eyes of a wild cat
gleaming on me from the bottom of the gallery.
My Nubian servant wept like a child.
While I considered what to do,
it rushed between my legs;
tumbling over mummies, dodging pits,
escaped into the air.

X I

I wear a ring in his image,
the shape and colour of immortality.
Crudded,
fallen off wheels,
fat under earth hardened by beggars' spit
the scarab's delighted;
or patting
his pillow inside a camel's
offal.
If I have to pass that
brownblack
at the stink, say, of noon,
I cross the street: I stare
as though the dung beetle were
performing
obscenities for my sake.

Norwegian Spring

I arrived there early in the morning—
the housemaid snoring down the stairwell—
to find the right room at the back of the hotel,
taking a courtyard blackened by pigeons;
pushed the door open, looked at
your tossed corpse and said, I'm glad
you couldn't get from Oslo to Bergen
without my love: I remember what holiness
humped my wings like a church with a curved prow;
resurrected every day, rose singing.
I was a row of houses whiter than sailors,
an eyelash in a zoo, the breast of the palace.
A butcher's knife cut off my belt,
a soldier got my shoes.
I moved all summer naked among thieves.
Birds on the fjords, birds everywhere in the world
could dive into the sea and not be drowned.

Jamaican Ministry

for Hugh Morrison

Father on horseback wouldn't arrive till sunset
In a whirl of mosquitoes
Under the thirty foot poinciana. I sniffed the rancid
Garden, counted the humming birds as their tongues
Milked the red flowers.
Derelict myrtle below their wings
Led to the mission porch where I would sit
Now, the new minister's son in a clean shirt.
Grass ribbed the floor.
And the humming birds, purple and bronze,
Ignored our shouts, footfalls.
My cousins took range
While the birds made blue fire, a faultless
Burning in midair.
We never saw their wings move,
Not even when we raised our slingshots.
A halo nearer earth than heaven
Ringed our heads:
Then birds fell, two, three, ten, eleven.
My cousins, hard in their vigor,
Kicked the bodies hurtling at their feet.
Who would think such feeble rigor mortis
A dolphin's rainbow or the last amenities
An old lady glows with? The ineffable feathers
Darkened, iridescence gone,
A coat of mail effaced to dun.
Heavy along the sky a simplicity like death
Lit the dry sun. Besieged,
My hand felt red, my wrist was burning.
I walked toward the house, suddenly mourning
A ghost too small to imagine.

The Great Auk

for Pierre and Janine Emmanuel

a

Count Raben at his country house, Aalholn, Nysted, Laaland:
"I own a badly stuffed auk, well-preserved."
The story of an extinct bird begins with the count's daughters,
Good housekeepers in a sunlight usually kept spotless.
The birds and the countesses had never met formally
And the old countess could hardly be expected to know about
the final extinction
On the skerry named Eldey, off the coast of Iceland.

b

"My father worked for your father, sir,
When the planets kept to their quarters,
Arranged the years in glass cases.
Every instrument of torture had a proper place
In the gallery, its particular dream
Of order."

c

A scholar writes, "It excites to pity,"
Kitchen middens accumulate.
Girls on beaches
Flick lights in windows. A vanished race
Shifts in our mind, we remember,
Although somewhere on the surface troubled
By the surprising beauty of a few facts
Like the seven birds killed by an Icelandic peasant
On the rock under Lautrum-Fugleberg.

d

1838–
a Danish journal warned readers: "for instance, the dront."
To names like that
Hudson added the white spoonbill, the egret, the capercaillie,
avocet, red
night-reeler, craking reed-wren among interlaced sedge blades.
In the Cattegut in the rictus of
thunder, men swear the auk has been seen waltzing
miraculously at nightfall,
as if you had been holding your breath
all this time.
Open up. A stunted wing
hangs half out of
your mouth, a hole disappearing into itself, exigent.
Step along. A comic
flurry of wings: the Holy Ghost, no bigger than a goose turd,
drops at your feet.

e

On fourteen stations remains have been recovered:
Saint Kilda, Orkney, Shetland, the three
Garefowl rocks, Danell's island situated
In latitude 65 20'N,
Gunntjornskjoerne. Sanctus, sanctus.
Alteration of the Gulf Stream
Compelled the Vikings to leave Greenland,
Harried the birds, who migrated toward Saint Lawrence.

The wind proves our exile. You might say we wandered,
Have died.

f

Sir Humphrey Gilbert's expedition to Newfoundland
Reported its habits in 1583:
It took pride in confining sallies within
The surf of a familiar village. Sailors,
Fishermen attest the constant friendliness:
Each bird persisted in fawning upon his murderer,
Seemed to ignore the disappearance of the others.

g

Audubon said the fishermen said the captain said
The auk still bred upon a low, rocky islet to the southeast of
   Newfoundland
Where great numbers of the young were once destroyed
   for bait.
The merest observation will populate imagination.
Ontogeny, philogeny: to exist is a triumph.

h

In those days garefowl frequented less isolated regions

   bowed to each other unmolested
   read seams of scaurs   the Scriptures

     we planted crops sideways

95

at other periods of the year did not leave soundings

    fed in shallow water

except when casting hope on long beaks   stubborn sea journeys

    swam   head lifted   neck drawn in

        a son contradicting his father

    never flapped the water
    but in alarm dived
    to drop down two fathoms off a cliff

whales   gulls   close sails passed them casually

        perhaps busy with children or grinding spearheads
        in the fastness of our mountain
        no whale no gull no sail

indifference being a form of joy

    sometimes uttered a low croak
    would not defend their eggs
    but fought fiercely
    if caught

        pledged that the enemy should not get us alive but

        generally as we confess
        easygoing hand to mouth

walk or run with short steps

and stand straight like a man.

                                    i

          As we approached
          along the narrow cliffs
          they were tight-rope walkers,
          their brief wings extended.
          Siguror and Ketil
          seized husband and wife
          by the rim of the boulder,
          a precipice a mile high.
          It reminded us of the time
          we enticed one to the side of the boat
          by holding out a few fish;
          then struck it with an oar,
          killed it outright, confidence
          to match our own:
          excessively stupid or
          insatiable
          and like the eye of a dead
          whale, not funny.

                                    j

Length of the bird to the end of its toes, three feet.
From the bill to the corner of the mouth, four inches
     and a quarter,

Strong, compressed, marked with several furrows
That tally both above and below,
Upper mandible covered with short, black velvetlike feathers;
Neck, back, tail, and wings a glossy black.
When supplied with food it was fond of,
stroked head with foot;
In a state of freedom, fed upon *cottus scorpius*,
Cyclopterus lumpus, the lumpfish.
Prophecies from Scorpio fill the night.
Stomach of a young bird captured in August
Contained roseroot which grows on ledges and crevices
   of seacliffs
Almost to within reach of the waves at highwater.

k

You can believe, I suppose,
This beautifully executed plate.
Look, the bird sitting on snow-covered
Ice of great thickness above an ice
Hole, the background filled in
With mountains of ice.
Peasants thought it blind
On land. A writer who flourished
Two centuries ago succeeded
In taming several birds:
But they died abruptly inland.

l

No one lands at Eden without a gun.

There is such plenty that unless a man took aim

he would think it an incredible thing.
"There are a thousand folde, as many
    hovering about it
        as within;

        black and white with beakes like unto crowes.
We named them *aporeth*"

                                    m

"Being flead off we dressed and eate them, their skinnes were like
honey combes, full of holes, but we found them to be good
                                    and nourishing
meate." So pacing the shore observed thousands, their bodies
                                    not removed
of which the fat were excellent fuel—the smell notwithstanding—
although feathers undecorative. Two now in England, prepared
                                    as skeletons
(one in the British Museum), each, unfortunately, missing
                                    several bones;
a deficiency eventually made up through the
kindness of Mr. J. Hancox of Philadelphia who extracted similar
members from a skin in his possession.

                                    n

The birds remembered
    into Thy hands
Hakluyt's voyage;
    I commend
driven to their death

                    without persuasion
                    on a sail spread out
                    from the side of the ship
                    to the nearest shore;

       my spirit, o Lord;
    when the birds grew
    less plentiful

                        you forced them into
                        compounds, slaughtered them
                        with clubs, sticks.

                            o

    To eat their excrement
    Back and forth through the dining-room, reciting
    "It's good, it's good."
    Ordered his dog to bite; the dog refusing,
    Hit the dog so hard it vomited.
    Obliged to eat the vomit;
    That afternoon twelve thousand corpses.
    If you want the skin tatooed,
    Better to hold their heads under water.
    At Birkenau herded the children together
    With clubs, sticks,
    Punctured their veins
    To see how much air needed
    Embolism.

p

To fly overland: to survive
The sheer weight of your body.
Summer has the sound
Of snow falling, of great
Winds, there in the middle of the heat.
Love is exact, will never fear
A shell, a fragile nest.
Garefowls laid one egg a year:
How long should love last?
On the Virgin Rocks, if you sit
Not too near the edge, midway
Along the northeast side of the spit,
A garefowl may still lie hidden.
Remembering what knowledge you have,
How to be a bird.

q

Take one example, captive, emaciated.
In a few days she became sprightly,
Plentifully supplied with fresh fish,
Permitted to dive with a cord attached to one of her legs;
Performed the motions of swimming under water,
A rapidity which set pursuit from a boat at defiance.
When the yacht harboured,
Being allowed her usual bath,
Escaped,
Which was a reasonable way of dying.

The colour of the inside of the mouth is said to have been yellow,
The nostrils a soul: but here the derivation
is inexact.
Geirr, Icelandic for spear,
As if we thought them arrogant.
Geier, German for vulture,
Indiscriminate hunger.
An island of birds
Ringed with a bank of ice,
At the centre an incredible happiness: broken and cracked
To the eye, harsh to the ear.

Picked up on a white shore,
A long way from where I live,
What had been an auk's midriff,
And held the v between my fingers.
Since those who inflict suffering become
What suffers, equal in ignorance
Before the hard tissue under the flesh.
It was Irony that spoke my prayer for me:
The lizard when it is blind in its old age
Creeps into the crevice of a wall
Facing toward the east and stretches out
Its head to the rising sun
Whose rays restore its sight.

In like manner seek thou the wall of help
And watch there till the Dayspring rise.

t

There is little hope now for the truth:
So few bones of the bird are left.

The Shapelifters

for Marcus and Bridget Worsley

"I speak of the passing of the soul at
death into another body or successive
bodily form, either human or animal."
Aleister Crowley

1.

This body, old fur, ferret, hides
In a withered room, defies
Mountains, lies
Close to valleys, but guides
A black claw to the left
Or right of them, never
Caught in holes: soundings discover
The depth of a cave, sift
An echo from the wall
And hold it to the ear. Wings fall
From my bed to the floor, then out to the level
Air, a bat in the shape of a devil.

2.

In Rome alectryomancy
meant dancing the way grass grows,
sidewise, to spread a handful,
a hatful of corn on the sand,
to throw a fit, be the sun
tracing an alphabet in the bushes,
flicker among midday moons
when the priest had knelt to the chicken
in her blowzy skirt and jaded rump,
smiling, oiling the frilly omen
which pecked a message in ¾

time, a slaughter of clouds
inhuman as hello, old widow,
or goodnight, earth: the flying
shadow of a rock.
Jump, you cock-hungry bird,
the dumbest soldier heard
your heart go chicken.

3.

We held his feet,
stood over him
exorcising
the demon on his brain.
"Out! out! get out."
He clucked like a hen;
suddenly he smiled,
his feet stopped writhing.
A herd of swine
rushed headlong
down our lawn and
into the sea.

4.

The river
echoing
what rides
the river:
my name
on the water,
the gilded

barge of
a cliché.
In a locked
bedroom
the carpet
also
ripples,
the body
shuffling
against the
body's
double:
a bald I
with a blind me;
no sound
possible
to describe
the bull with Io,
the swan with
Leda.

5.

I am born at midnight by incantation,
   bajang, bajang,
When the train has crushed in the crowded station
And the town burns down and the polecats fashion
   bajang, bajang
In their blazing eyes the hunter on his mustang,
   bajang, bajang.

6.

This stone has two eyes, this trunk
Has two arms, this chain wears a smile,
These bracelets have tongues of fire.

106

They will sail down the Xingu on soft feet
And kill everyone they meet.

7.

The fox is
a malicious lady
who lives
to a great age
and is beautiful in bed
at a hundred.

8.

When I went out on Lismore,
On Lismore on the green,
All I had was my old gun
And a gold doubloon.

When I went out on Lismore
As far as Balnagown,
One fat hare was all I saw
Running up and down.

When I went out on Lismore
The hare began to scream:
Shoot me, darling, shoot. But first
Give me back my name.

9.

A jaguar with the coming of night.
This feline alter ego,
brujo,
lifting the teapot:
stop talking.

1 0.

"... but I tell you
I *do* turn into a panther.
No, I can't
do it for you now,
can't do it like that
whenever I want.
Something
happens to me
but when it happens
I *am* a
panther."

1 1.

I give the fleas an IQ test
to see their reflexes.
That's the way I pick my trainees.
They catch the meaning of words,
juggle balls, pull carts, climb ladders.
I use breezes, odors
to show them what's expected of them.
If flies are the devil's familiars
fleas are the guardians of the intellect.

1 2.

I am Giles Garnier.
Garnier is my name.
My old man was Garnier,
Garnier my old dame.

I can read in church;
I'm a firstclass host.
Mourners will be dozens
When I fall to dust.

Some men call me simple,
Others call me wise.
Sons have called me father:
Kissed me on the eyes.

I am Giles Garnier,
Garnier is my name.
My old man was Garnier,
My wife the same.

> (Garnier: *loup garou* who prowled at dark,
> seized, killed and mangled children,
> ate them raw; put to the rack, confessed;
> was burned at the stake).

1 3.

Mary Hatt at her doorway:
quick, call the doctor,
call the police.
Dust swirling from the lid of the grand piano,
a bowl of roses overturned in the hall.
Quick, call the priest.
A window half open,
the best chair upside down.
On a neighbor's rosebush a spider
spelled
her name
in spiderweb.

1 4.

Apollonius:
recently dead and much-mourned king,
yellow mane in the yellow sun, you return to roar
green blessings upon us, herbivorous, gentle.

	your red holes have water in them
Jesus:	for a pledget of Lent to put against the heart.
	ravenous claw slipped under the dry
Pliny:	earth now, your soul is squeezed from
	your mouth in the maw of a raven.

1 5.

There grew a morning she was tired.
It would not go away.
  The light that hurt her eyes was black,
  She saw the sunlight sway.

   There rose a night when he lay down,
   Down he was all day:
   My love, he said, if I could move,
   God knows, I would not stay.

And so she went to where he lay,
Her bush soul to his butterfly.

1 6.

Love me love my cat, not really
a slogan with nine lives. Maybe you took it
out of the car trunk, threw away the collar,
hoped he would get lost, probably starve.
So poison the water, call the cat bad names,
shut him in an attic in Pisa:
this room stank three hundred years of cat
that is, turds and piss, just below the tower.
Say you cut off the whiskers, burnt
the left eyebrow with a cigarette,
stepped hard on his tail, kicked it:
do you think anyone would die?

1 7.

But the facts are, horses rapped out with their hooves clear
answers to simple questions, complex mathematical formulas;
one horse was blind, could not be influenced by light;
another very young, a third very old. They were without
control, no one being in the stables.

1 8.

I leave to Blake my angels,
To Yeats my sparkling hunter;
Wordsworth has my hilltop
With the sun dead center;
So to every poet
Blessings or a gift
(But here, and there in heaven
My curse upon you, Swift).

1 9.

We lit a fire,
The door of our tent looked out on it,
Our supper was cooking on it.
Horses and mules, tethered in a semicircle,
Turned that way and blinked at it.
Far off, a jackal saw it and barked;
It drew us all together.
Its smoke went quietly up
Toward the stars.

Babylonian Astronomy

They counted the distance a man travelled between fear and hope:
Nineteen miles from the moon to the Pleiades,
Fourteen miles from Orion to Sirius;
And so on, through eight constellations, always asking
How far one god eclipsed others.
Their minds boggled at what might happen
Behind a cloud.

Every courtyard led toward a fountain
The color of the Milky Way.
To close the door too loud
Could sound like the disappearance of a planet
As you walked around the block
And sank home drunk before sunrise.
The shutting off of light from one celestial body
By the intervention of another
Resembled love in a hanging garden at midnight.

the day begins a long way out in the country

you take off your skin
and there are no mirrors   (you cannot say
                where the light falls it hurts)
                                        your feet
watching themselves
                as they lean forward
sink among the dense tufts
sunlight lengthens
                picking out each blade
stretches   (not like pain)
                heavy
                        against the mounds of pebble
a feather floats down
nothing can catch it
it holds a giant's immunity
                with the persistence of
                                stone
the shadow between two bushes
                becomes a bush
                oleanders are smaller magnolias
                coarser azaleas more subtle
                this flowering brake at the edge of an
                                                eyelid
                flooded with blooms louder than water
                                        has no name
beyond it in the auburn field brindled
cows shift their black lights through the broken
stalks
                as far as the reticence of
                evergreens shrunken to the amenities of
                perpetual old age
                underneath them
                the sun turns granite into
                                        dust

there's no violence in the hot noon
        except a boulder
        buried by grass
        filled by an antique dung
                richer than gold
The corn stubble's
        growing
            new legs
            moving just enough to be
            yellow
overhead the crows
        scream
        because they can fly
        branches bend freighted with
                    beaks and claws
                    a remote possibility of
                    hunger
the cows cough gently
        too much sand
        bothers the leaves
        clean tails whipping horseflies keep time
                      to invisible music
neither beautiful nor deep
the field leads nowhere
gathers no hills
touches
        no lake
            has no horizon
it reaches a highway coiled
        to strike at your ankles
faintly across the heaviness of the sky
a man whistles from his truck
        so distant
        it is

lost among mocking-birds
a world of
                wheels
                sighs with precision in the heat

as if a young girl wrapped in veils
or an old woman after fifty years
                stared at her body
knowing that this was not
                her body
felt satisfied
                to be a wing
                            among flowers

A Song for Innocence

for Neyan Watts Stevens

O desolate spring in the middle of the desert,
We have walked down the green margins of the hills
And come across the sand in the short
Cool hours when the heart fills
With love, hoping to find your clear
Waters under the fruit of the oasis
Which the cowboy sang about.
A promise
Led us over the burning dunes
Hour after hour, year after year until
We forgot our thirst.
At last we are lost and drink
Dry air with a few curses. There is nothing to think;
Our eyes grow blind, our feet no longer
Remember where they were going or why
We began: only, inside us, each carries gratefully the cry
Of the others like food from a stranger
Whose ignorance is our home, whose body
Lying in the desert is our body.

The VCU Series for Contemporary Poetry was founded as a joint publication between Virginia Commonwealth University, the Associated Writing Programs, and the University Press of Virginia in order to establish a means by which poets could recommend to other poets, publishers, and readers collections of contemporary verse which they believed to be outstanding and deserving immediate publication.

For the 1975 series, twenty-three poets from every area of the country read over one thousand manuscripts submitted to them by both young and established American and Canadian poets. Of these thousand manuscripts, a hundred and twenty-six were recommended by the initial readers to a second committee, composed of R. H. W. Dillard, George Garrett, James B. Hall, William Peden, James Whitehead, and Miller Williams. These readers, in turn, selected thirteen collections which were passed to the final judge, Richard Eberhart, who chose five which he felt possessed the highest literary excellence and ought to be published immediately. They were by David Walker, Robert Huff, Leon Stokesbury, Richard Moore, and David Posner.

Each year, the University Press of Virginia and other interested presses publish as many of the collections chosen through this procedure as financially possible, with the aim of encouraging poets and exposing readers to the best contemporary literature. Manuscripts are accepted in the fall of each year, and inquiries are welcomed through the editor. Write: Walton Beacham, VCU Series for Contemporary Poetry, Virginia Commonwealth University, Richmond, Virginia 23284